READ TODAY, SELL TOMORROW

How to Sell, Sell, Sell…

John Mepham

ISBN
13:978-1491015681

ABOUT THE AUTHOR

When you read any book you are not confident in its contents unless you are sure that the author really knows the subject of that book. You will be particularly concerned if the book is a textbook, a do-it-yourself book or similar. To give you confidence in READ TODAY, SELL TOMORROW and its author I trust that you will allow me just a little brag.

I was Managing Director for some twenty-two years of a public property company with a quote on the London Stock Exchange. Also, for ten years I was a partner in a firm of surveyors and estate agents; before retirement I was a Chartered Surveyor.

I bought and sold all types of property throughout southern England and negotiated at the highest level. That market is one of the most exacting markets in the world.

My record proves that I have the confidence and experience to put this book before you.

JOHN MEPHAM

INTRODUCTION

Carefully read these twenty-five guidelines. They are composed to get your thoughts and actions moving in the right direction. Adapt them to your own circumstances. Think and act in the suggested manner and soon your own personal guidelines will replace them. At that stage you will be on your way to a more fulfilling and prosperous life and career. I had to fight hard to keep these guidelines concise. I was tempted to write a lot more. That would have defeated my aim of providing an easy-to-read book for busy people. You haven't the time to read all the academic theory which is provided in so many how-to-do-it books. That is not provided here. You do not need it. You need pithy advice that you will benefit you on most days.

You will soon realise that I like quotations. I find that a good quotation helps one to remember. An apt quotation sticks in the memory. I do hope that you like the quotations and that they will help you to remember the lessons that these guidelines set out to teach.

WHY THE TITLE?

The reason is straightforward. Read this book today and, from the tips that you receive from its contents you will be able to profitably sell tomorrow. That is the aim of this book. That is why the book is concise - it will not waste your time.

Go directly into the marketplace and earn money. It may sound too simple - try it and you may well be amazed at what you achieve.

I present this book in a time-saving manner as your aim is to get ahead in your profession, business or trade without any delay. You do not want to waste time reading a lengthy academic treaty. If those last two sentences are truly relevant to you, then you are on your way to a worthwhile career and these twenty-five mandatory actions (known as MA`s hereafter) were written for you.

Of course, you will often be buying and these MA`s will help you in that important activity.

ONE – NOTHING HAPPENS UNLESS YOU MAKE IT

That has always been my personal motto. It must be realised that there is little difference between an opportunity and an obstacle. Think that an obstacle stops an opportunity - and it will. Think and act on a way of removing an obstacle and an opportunity is likely to come to light. You see, you can make things happen, but YOU must take action. As said in King Lear, **"Nothing comes out of nothing".** So, next time you consider that you merit a wage rise, do something about it - go and see the boss. The first action must always be YOURS, otherwise you won`t get that rise. Do nothing - and nothing good is likely to happen. Make this MA your personal motto. **Take this MA to heart and both remember and use it in your everyday life/work. It is fundamental to you success.**

TWO - NEVER HAVE TO SIGH, "IF ONLY..."

If you do not take MA ONE to heart it may well be that your future will be of many "If only..." episodes. You will look back in resentment. You won`t be able to do anything about that past episode, but you can - and must - prepare so as to avoid future "If only" predicaments. Constantly call to mind MA ONE and show a belief in yourself by becoming a doer, an action man - not just a thinker/dreamer hoping that it will all turn out to your advantage; of course, unless you are very lucky, it won`t.

Start at once on improving your working day and put realistic ideas into action - do not delay. A negotiator/salesperson must be a doer - that is a fine thought to "kick start" you into action.

Do not only plan ahead. Be active today and your future will look after itself. Don`t be pleased with second best, the majority of people achieve that every day. Believe - genuinely believe - that good negotiators/salespersons will, without a shadow of doubt, get ahead of the herd and will rarely have to sigh, "If only...".

A thought: It is so easy to kid yourself that all your tomorrows will be fine. You just sit back and wait - but, for what? That question brings you right back to MA ONE. In reality, kidding yourself is doing nothing and we now know where that gets us - nowhere.

A challenging command to be obeyed if you don`t want to sigh, "If only..." in the future - **begin to build your future TODAY., there is no alternative.**

<u>THREE</u> - YOU MUST KNOW WHAT YOU SEEK

It is of little use going on a journey without knowing the destination. Doesn`t that apply to life? To get the best out of life you must have an objective - a target, a goal. Ok., I hear you. That generally means making some money - that is an honourable aim. Good, you have an ambition. You must have or create a burning desire to reach your target and that burning desire will force and entice you into considering how to hit the bulls eye.

Everyone lives by selling something be it goods, services, advice (your brains), charm, humour, wit, et al. It follows that only by using negotiating/sales tactics will you truly succeed. Here is a concrete example of that. Assume that you want to be a butcher. You have to buy meat (negotiating) and sell it (salesmanship). A few pounds off the buying price and a few pounds on the selling price and you are pounds in. Get it? Look at your personal objective/s and see how negotiating/salesmanship can improve both your everyday work and your life generally.

Einstein said, **"I never think of the future. It comes too soon."** You see, wise Einstein proclaims that there is no time to waste. The future is just around the corner. You know what you seek - start to find it **NOW;** otherwise, time will slip away and you may well have to find an unprofitable refuge in MA TWO. Now, that should shock you into action

FOUR – ALWAYS DISPLAY THE RIGHT ATTITUDE

How do you appear to others? Or, more to the point, how **should** you appear to them? It will ruin your cause if you project an abrasive image. No one likes a brash loudmouth show-off. Do you? Such a person is generally endeavouring to hid ignorance and appears ill at ease. That is fatal.

You must relax, smile and be patient and listen, especially when under pressure. Then, your confidence will shine through without any false display. However, do not push either yourself or your cause by being too eager or hurried. Relax and give a good impression. It is useful to keep in mind this Arab proverb: **Patience is the key to joy. Haste is the key to sorrow.** Now, that is prudent advice. Store it in your memory bank.

The ideal - be seen as a relaxed and patient person. That will say it all. It will show the image of a person who undoubtedly knows what he is talking about. If you project that image you will be well on the way to success.

In what way do so many persons go wrong? They pretend to be "Mr Big". They look silly, weak and insecure. No one believes them. Be yourself that is the only way to impress those that you meet.

There is a comparatively easy way to discovery incorrect attitudes. It is interesting and can be profitable to see how others act. You will soon learn that certain attitudes and/or actions annoy you. They are likely to have the same result on others. If you possess any of those annoying attitudes immediately endeavour to eliminate them from your make-up.

When you speak you give much away in addition to the words that you utter. To give the correct attitudes remember these five themes. (1) Keep it simple. Avoid long and complicated dissertations. Talk so that the listener clearly hears and understands what you are putting across. Summarise in a simple sentence or two, preferably just before you stop talking. Leave the listener with a clear message. (2) Do not get lost. Use your notes as a surreptitious guide, so that an essential detail is not forgotten. (3) Be yourself. Do not attempt to be the type of person that you think your listener wants to hear. You won`t get away with acting. (4) As so often mentioned in these MA`a - relax. That will show that you are confident, know your job and enjoy talking about it. That will please the listener and put him in a receptive mood. (5) Try not to read from notes. To be seen as spontaneous will help to show that, without any prompting, you know the score. These five actions will be of great assistance in promoting the right attitude when you speak.

<u>FIVE</u> – ALWAYS REMEMBER THAT "MANNERS MAKETH THE MAN"

You have realised the truth of MA FOUR and are doing your best to project the right image. That`s fine. Don`t spoil it by a display of bad manners. That will ruin all the beneficial work done to date.

The use of bad language is both pointless and extremely harmful. It signifies that you are losing control and that you don`t really know how to proceed. It is a smoke screen in which you seek to hide your lack of knowledge of the subject being discussed. Never fall into that trap.

Other displays of bad manners which must be avoided are being bossy (that`s a sure loser), being rude (that`s a perfect way to start an unproductive slanging match) and being arrogant (that will guarantee that you will be disliked). You see, every act of bad manners will have a detrimental outcome and you will be the one who suffers.

To sum-up: Good manners can be expressed in just three words - ALWAYS BE POLITE. Bad manners gain nothing and lose a lot. It is as simple as that. **Remember - a bout of bad manners will put your blood pressure up, not your opponent`s.**

<u>SIX</u> - EVERYONE WISHES TO WORK WITH A REASONABLE PERSON

It is futile being in any way unreasonable. In particular, that is relevant to what you seek - your ultimate aim. Two typical examples: Firstly, if the market salary for your job is £20,000 per annum, you are wasting everyone`s time by seeking £30,000 per annum. You are being unreasonable and greedy. Secondly, if your house has been valued at circa £250,000 the market will laugh - and do nothing else - if you ask £350,000. Again, you are being unreasonable and greedy.

To be greedy is to be unreasonable. Who wants to do a deal or be friendly with an unreasonable person? In the examples given it will completely shatter your case and you will not get a rise or sell your house. You see, your greed will rebound on you.

If you become known as an unreasonable person no one will want to deal with you. Of course, deals will be done, but your work will be made that much more difficult. People soon sense an unreasonable person and, remember, news travels fast.

Be believable, practicable, rational, sensible, equitable, likeable... all elements of being a reasonable person.

A word of warning: Never underestimate yourself. You may - you probably are - better than you think. It is not unreasonable to tactfully display your ability. Do not go too far and become conceited, boastful or just a verbal show-off It is unreasonable to be a tedious windbag.

It is important to remember that a reasonable person is often considered to be of sound judgment.

SEVEN – WHEN SELLING NEVER ARGUE OR ROW

When you reason you are trying to open a closed mind. The very word "reason" brings to mind "being reasonable" as set out in the last MA. Only reason can open a closed mind. You don't argue, have a row or stop anyone from having their say. Quite the contrary. You use your knowledge together with your negotiating skills to quietly, persistently and pleasantly destroy the case against you and to advance your own. To do otherwise is likely to tighten an already closed mind.

You must listen, otherwise you won't clearly hear the case against you. Never say, "I'm right" or "You're wrong" (it may be true, but don't be that honest). Give the complete story (you may not have another opportunity) and find some area/s of agreement at an early stage; that will show that you are reasonable and willing to deal. These are effective weapons to clear away unimportant matters as soon as possible. Then, you can move forward with some mutual understanding under your belts. Maybe the agreed matters are insignificant ones, nevertheless you have some agreement and that must be a plus.

Do not be over eager. To be so will show that you can't do without whatever you are endeavouring to gain. The result of that eagerness will surely be that you will not get the best of any agreement struck. Bernard Shaw went straight to the point when he said to William Morris, **"If you want a thing you will always get the worst of a bargain"**. GBS was saying - don't SHOW your desire, it will cost you. Of course, you would not be in negotiation if you did not require what you are endeavouring to obtain - the lesson is this, do not **show** an over eagerness. Again, it pays to be reasonable.

An amusing thought to keep in your memory bank - never wrestle with the chimney sweep.

You see, negotiating/salesmanship is reasoning. That is all that it is...plus explaining, persuading and getting the wished for result!! Here are two words to sum it up - **ceaselessly explain.** Believe it or not that was Lenin`s motto.

To survive in the world of bargaining and dealing you must ascertain what the other side genuinely want and why. You work - that is, reason - on that information. It is useless trying to sell something that is not required. Some experts on the subject say create a need and endeavour to fill it. Ok., if your company is one of the "big boys" and your efforts are backed by a mega advertising programme. That is another story. An average company with much less funds will find it hard work to create a need. So, try and do it the other way round and show - reason - that your goods or services will meet an urgent EXISTING need.

EIGHT - BE POSITIVE AND ELIMINATE THE NEGATIVE

The words of a favourite song of mine give this sound advice, "You`ve got to accentuate the positive, eliminate the negative..." That is a wonderful way of remembering this MA. If you are negative or pessimistic it will show and it will be used against you. A truly positive negotiator is a lethal opponent and will, at the very least, depress and dismay an opponent. In all life "accentuate the positive" and be in the right frame of mind to "take on the world".

To take another step forward - a positive person will become an optimist and an opportunist. That is, flexible in outlook, an expert in the art of improvisation and willing to grab every opportunity that arises. Consider that last statement - it`s quite the reverse of turning down every suggestion and idea or being faintly negative when you are more or less forced to be positive. Do you get it? Travel hopefully and as the song says "eliminate the negative". Of course, sometimes you have to say or do something that is not positive. But, you only do that when there is absolutely no alternative. Then, make the negative sound as attractive as possible.

Did you know that your own resolve to succeed is more important than any other incentive? You are, in effect, challenging yourself to succeed. You will do all in your power not to let yourself down. That is a helpful thought.

NINE - GET MOTIVATED

What is your motive? Let`s be frank, it is being successful which predominantly means only one thing - to make as much money as is possible. A perfectly honourable aspiration.

You must keep that motive well to the fore. Without a motive you will remain in a rut. With it you will keep going. Just like perpetual motion - once started it goes on and on and on.In your mind you will be conditioning yourself to knowing that the battle is being won. It is a battle, a very ferocious battle, for it is you against a multitude of others all trying to hit a target similar to yours. Go into any supermarket or look along any high street on a busy Saturday afternoon and you will see swarms of people - a large percentage of whom will be in some way or another your competitors. You see, many, many competitors really do exist. A suggested slogan to remind you of this fact - If I don`t grab the opportunity there are many others just waiting for me to slip.
Other motivations that are part of the wider field include wanting to improve your family`s well-being; In sport, wanting to be the best cricketer or footballer in your team; In estate agency, wanting to have more "sold by" boards displayed on the streets than competitors; In law, wanting to win the case... and there are hundreds more motivations that will be the starting point of success. Compare this MA with MA THREE.

REMEMBER THE GREATEST AID TO SUCCESS IS TO GET MOTIVATED

TEN - IT IS EASY TO THINK ONLY OF YOURSELF. THE OTHER PERSON IS HUMAN. TREAT HIM AS SUCH AND GIVE A HELPING HAND

You must give the other person a helping hand in the sense that you politely and surreptitiously guide him towards your goal. You do not crush the opponent by shouting down all views put forward. Here are some useful phrases: "I understand your point of view, but let us consider this as a possible compromise…", "Please correct me if I am wrong…", "That is a difficult question, may I deal with it later?", "Let me see if I understand what you are saying…". You see, you never say directly, "You are wrong". Everyone likes to be right and will fight like a tiger to the bitter end to prove it when challenged in the wrong manner. You must "reason" your opponent away from that possible predicament. Don`t get his back up by being provocative that won`t help either of you.

Your opponent may be like a boiler that is out of control and about to burst. In such a state, like the boiler, he will be dangerous and threatening. Let him let off steam and, thereafter, you will be dealing with a more comfortable person. The moral is this - like you, others have views to put forward, hear them. If you show an interest in others they will repay you by showing an interest in you. Now, that`s a fair bargain.

An effective approach which clearly shows that you are not only thinking of yourself is to explain that your opponent wants this and you want that - so, let`s find a compromise. I don`t like the "half-way bargain" but this idea could well be the start of a useful discussion. Bernard Shaw said, **"Treat everyone as an equal"**. Now, that is a lesson on which to end this MA.

ELEVEN - TALK TO A PERSON WHO CAN GIVE AN UNQUALIFIED DECISION

Do not waste time and effort (that is real energy being used up) by talking to the wrong person - someone who can only pass a message on to a superior. For example, if you seek a pay rise only go to the boss - the person who finds the money to pay you. To go to a manager, who has little or no say in the financial affairs of the business, is pointless. You will only get, "I`ll speak to the boss". Someone else will be putting your case for a rise and that can`t be right.

When selling to a firm go to the Sales Director who is likely to be able to place a firm order. To put goods in front of an assistant will be allowing that person to sell your goods to the Sales Director. Again, that can`t be right.

A truism - only YOU can really and truly present YOUR case in its best light. You have the desire to succeed. To an intermediate it is just another job. Why should he fight your battle? You must do your own reasoning as, you know all the facts and figures. No one else can do your job as efficiently as you. Constantly think the sentiment expressed in that last sentence.

A proviso - of course, it may well be that it is just not possible to speak to the right person. You could write, but that doesn`t have the same impact. Being a person who rarely gives in you seek a person who has influence with that right person and persuade him to put your case. That is not an ideal situation. Nevertheless, if you can trace a person of whom you believe has influence, it might just be worthwhile. At least, you have tried and that is the action of a true doer

Remember – it is a waste of time to talk to an underling who is likely to pass on your message in an uninterested manner.

In all negotiating/sales situations you must always try all angles before giving up. Nonetheless, time must not be wasted and you must move on from a lost cause immediately you realise that there is little hope of a successful outcome. To know that moment is one of the traits of a first-class negotiator/salesperson.

TWELVE - A PLAN OF ACTION IS VITAL

Be like a Boy Scout - **be prepared.** That is another worthy slogan to retain in your memory bank.

The disorganised person is too busy being disorganised to get the very best out of his work and of life generally. To go to a meeting with only a vague idea of how you are going to put your case is the certain way to disaster. You are not prepared, you deserve to be humiliated. It is not an atom of good blaming anyone else - be utterly truthful and blame yourself. Before a meeting - yes, you must find the time - work out a plan. Just a few brief notes are better than nothing. The very act of putting notes on paper helps to concentrate the mind and you will reason in a more structured manner.

Here is an example of brief notes written before a meeting. You are seeking to purchase a smallish area of land to extend your garden. You are going to meet your neighbour in an endeavour to agree terms. Your notes could look like this - (1) Discuss the area - size - you wish to purchase. (2) Explain that the fine Elm tree will not be destroyed. (3) Point out why the neighbour`s bungalow will not suffer from loss of light, view, etc. (The value may well be reduced more than the price being obtained for the land - but, that is not your problem). (4) You will provide at your cost a new garden shed to replace the old one. (5) Having agreed all matters other than price that can now be brought into the discussions. You see, brief headings will keep all the important points before you. You will have no need to waffle.

A plan and brief notes are an absolute necessity

Of course, you may well be waylaid and have to deviate from the plan. That`s ok. The notes are still in front of you for guidance. You won`t forget any of those vital points. Your notes have, therefore, been of assistance

THIRTEEN - TIME MUST BE USED WISELY. NEVER WASTE IT. ONCE GONE IT IS LOST FOREVER

Time waits for no one - it is the most precious and perishable commodity you will come across. Whatever you do in life time is used to "reason" with people to do or not to do this or that. That is why this MA must never be ignored. For example, an agenda or your own plan will help to keep any meeting on course. Without that type of support all meetings drift, people will waffle, unconnected matters will be discussed...and so much irretrievable time will be wasted. Poorly organised meetings are the greatest time waster known to man.

Ponder this question - how much time do you waste every day? Look back at yesterday. Could you have achieved more at work with a simple plan or some rough guidance notes before you? Of course you could. So, as from NOW plan, as far as is practical, your working day and, to save more time, alter your plan as circumstances dictate. Be flexible and create time. Be stubborn and eliminate all thoughts and actions that waste working time. Then, you will find how easy it will be to find time for that extra round of golf! Don`t forget that a plan is your guide not your master; hence, if for any reason it gets in the way of a sudden business opportunity, cast it aside and plan for that new profitable opening.

Never waste business time

A useful suggestion - At the end of the working day make a note of matters that MUST be undertaken tomorrow. The vital ones that are (very) likely to lead to good business will be at the top of the list. You, who want a worthwhile future, waste none of the present.

The real lesson is this: a negotiator/salesperson must use as much time as possible creating and undertaking valuable business. The aim must be to reduce time spent on non-business producing work and use it to promote real profitable business. Of course, some routine work must be undertaken. Keep it to a minimum.

A thought - you may waffle, delay, dawdle, postpone, daydream, et al. That`s your privilege. Time will not await your attention. As Benjamin Franklin said, **"You may delay but time will not"**. That is a useful quote on which to end this MA.

FOURTEEN - NEVER GOSSIP, NATTER, WAFFLE OR PREACH. SPEAK IN A CLEAR MANNER WITH YOUR OBJECTIVE WELL TO THE FORE.

To gossip, natter, waffle, preach or similar is a complete waste of time and, more to the point, may provide the listener with ammunition to use against you. The more verbose, the more you disclose of your side of the possible bargain and of yourself. Keep strictly to the point.

Furthermore, to be verbose may give the impression that you have lost your way - you probably have! It stops the listener putting forward his case. Your continued chatter stops you from clearly hearing the other side of the story. Sooner or later your verbosity must cease.

You and your case are both exhausted. From that point on you have to listen to a reasonable case from a calm opponent who will use your views to help put forward his assertions. Your gossip, nattering, waffling, preaching, et al. has got you nowhere. What a waste of both time and energy.

Never waste time by talking too much.

Maybe you consider that you have the gift of the gab. That is fine, but do not let that gift turn you gabby. Do not let it get in the way of action. Use that gift to get your objective clearly across to the opponent. Otherwise, it is just a lot of wasted hot air.

A lesson to learn - Never disclose more than is strictly necessary. Brevity, so they say, is the art of speaking without giving anything away. Learn that art.

There was a war time saying - **careless talk costs lives**. Now, that is worth putting into your memory bank with "loses negotiations" instead of "costs lives".

All the chatter that you are warned about in this MA is, generally, talking in the incorrect way. However, not to waffle is so vital to your success that it needs an MA to itself.

<u>FIFTEEN</u> - DO NOT WAFFLE

Look up the word "waffle" in a dictionary and you will find that it is to speak aimlessly, ignorantly or in a vague manner. That confirms my idea of waffling as talking incessantly and/or nonsensically in a false endeavour to show that you have a strong grasp of the subject matter being discussed - when, in reality, you are completely lost and the listener knows full well of your discomfort. That description is proof that this MA must always be obeyed. Put yourself in the listener's shoes - interest completely lost and your effort is wasted. To quote a popular catch phrase, your words are going in one ear and out of the other. He knows that you are completely lost. Why should a listener even try to follow a waffler talking rubbish?

He who waffles is likely to be the loser.

To be realistic, it is possible that a waffler knows the subject but is not able to marshall the facts in a coherent form. That is nearly as harmful as being ignorant of the facts. The result is the same - the speaker is trying to cloak discomfort under a barrage of words. That will not work.

There is only one way to avoid waffling - comprehensively know your job, particularly the actual task in hand. Have a plan and keep to the point. To do otherwise is both futile and unproductive. That last word sums-up waffling.

SIXTEEN - STOP, LOOK, LISTEN AND OBSERVE. YOU MUST KNOW WHAT IS GOING ON

That brilliant observer Noel Coward said, **"I keep my eyes open, my ears open and my mouth shut".** That is a fine piece of advice. It is crucial that you know what is going on in the world around you and, as important, have some idea of what is likely to happen in the future. For example - Is the market stable or moving up or down? What are competitors doing? Is the new shop along the road doing much business? Is the boss well-placed to give me a rise? - and so on. You see, by not keeping up-to-date you may well miss an opportunity or put your foot in it. Not a desirable or pleasant achievement.

What you hear and observe is likely to provide the gist of reasoning when you endeavour to strike a bargain. You are not in an ivory tower; you are in the rough tough world with everyone else. So, always be fully prepared and use every possible occasion to stop, look, listen and observe and that will help to keep you well up-to-date.

To allow yourself to get out of date is to allow yourself to become a complete failure

SEVENTEEN – YOU MUST REMEMBER THAT VALUE AND PRICE ARE NOT ALWAYS THE SAME. CONVINCE THAT YOUR SALES PRICE EQUALS OR IS LOWER THAN VALUE AND YOU ARE WINNING

When you choose to sell an item you quote a price. That can be any figure that you choose. But, and here is the rub, unless the price is near the value of that item it is unlikely to be sold. Value being its relative worth compared with what similar items are now fetching in the market. Beware, the value of an article can, and does, go up and down and, in some situations, may vary from day-to-day. You must be observant. You now see how relevant MA SIXTEEN is to your success.

Look at this truism - a good trader/dealer sells at over value and buys at under value. That is how it works in an ideal world. Of course, no one operates in an ideal world. Nevertheless, keep that truism in mind as you negotiate.

That famous epigram said by Oscar Wilde sums-up this MA **"They know the price of everything, but the value of nothing"**. It is true that few persons know the REAL VALUE, but everyone you meet will know the price. So, talk value, impress upon the customer that your goods represent sound VALUE as compared with other similar items on offer. Better still, give examples. A potential customer will find it somewhat difficult to argue about real value; whereas, if you mention price he will give you a hundred and one examples of prices being asked by other traders.

With higher priced items the asking price is often increased so that part can be taken off when haggling. Be wary - don`t increase the price too much as that higher price may well put off potential customers. The best ploy has to be to keep an asking price as near true value as possible and work on that angle. Even when really desperate do not invite offers. That will show that you have no confidence in the asking price. Those two words "or offer" mean that you will not achieve the asking price.

A summary on the important elements of price and real value (1) Know the difference between price and real value. (2) Keep the real value of your goods/services before possible buyers. (3) Do not invite offers. Have confidence in your asking price.

EIGHTEEN – TAYLOR YOUR APPROACH TO THE STATE OF THE MARKET

It is absolutely necessary to know the market in which you work. You must match working conditions to the state of the market. Also, you must do your best to anticipate how the market is likely to proceed - is it stable or about to go up or down? Then, and only then, can you prepare for the better or worse conditions that are likely to come. Note those last five words. You must never bank on changing conditions, keep observing, keep on guard for you can never be certain that tomorrow`s conditions will be as predicted.

By assiduous observations you will learn to "read the market" and, hence, get and keep ahead of competitors. That sounds complicated. It is not really that difficult. As you progress in your chosen profession, business or trade you will learn every facet of that industry, that includes how sales are moving and how to price. You will get to know "the tricks of the trade". Look for and read and digest everything you can about your job. Read the relevant trade magazines and journals. Seek from your boss and others answers to questions that puzzle you. Never give up the search for information that will help you get ahead in your job. Taken together all that information that you are acquiring will give an overall background knowledge and you will soon learn to detect how the market and prices are likely to move.

Tips on dealing with different market conditions: IN A BOOM - adopt a "take-it-or-leave it" attitude. Be firm, always polite and reasonable. Imply that if terms can`t be agreed there are many others who will treat. Do remember that although that is (probably) true you have to spend time and money finding them - a bird in the hand. IN A SLUMP or demanding market conditions. This is a far more complicated situation. Everyone knows that everyone else is eager - perhaps desperate - to do business. You might argue that you detect that business is improving - give an example if at all possible. Emphasise value. If possible show that your terms are so much better than competitors, particular when quality is compared. Show that you are not desperate and seek a fair "today`s price" for your superior goods. Yes, of course, it becomes very grim when it looks as though there is not a realistic customer in sight. How you tackle that depends on the depth of the slump and your own financial circumstances but, do remember, that there are always opportunities out there. The only real remedy is to work very hard, see more possible customers, give good value for money and remain positive and optimistic. That sounds demanding. It is and is the only way to work in a recession/slump.

An amusing thought - don`t be a bear in a boom.

ONLY BY READING THE MARKET CORRECTLY WILL YOU BE ABLE TO TAKE FULL ADVANTAGES OF THE MOVEMENT OF PRICES

NINETEEN - NEVER BE CAUGHT IN A POSITION THAT ENTAILS LOSS OF FACE. KEEP AN ESCAPE HATCH OPEN

This MA is clear when expressed in this manner - never be manoeuvred into a position where there is no escape, where you have to admit that you are wrong or to do something else that damages your case. However, the remedy is not easy.

The obvious trap is when you have a weakness which a competitor can expose and benefit therefrom. The solution is that if you have a weakness expose it as soon as is possible. Get minor ones out of the way promptly. Do it by way of an example or in a jocular manner. If a weakness is fundamental to your objective it may well be that you shouldn`t have started the enterprise in the first place.

I call this exercise "keeping the escape hatch open". It entails preparing the ground in a competent and effective way so that you do not proceed with a venture containing a weakness. Look at every aspect of your reasoning and eliminate weaknesses and likely pitfalls. This is carried out as you prepare your plan/notes. That is the only sure way of not being ensnared without an escape hatch.

How many times have you been caught out and crossly said, under your breath, "I`ve given too much away and am now stuck with it". You see, you talked too much, gave a secret away and have no escape hatch. You have to make the best of a bad job. Learn from that example - if you want to be verbose always be cautious.

REMEMBER – ALWAYS HAVE AN "ESCAPE HATCH" READY FOR USE

TWENTY - WHEN GIVING AN ULTIMATUM – BE CAREFUL. IT IS A RISK. IF REFUSED YOU HAVE LOST THE INITIATIVE

In desperation you may be tempted to give an ultimatum. It could be, "Accept my offer by twelve noon tomorrow or the deal is off". That sounds pompous. It may be your downfall. What happens at five minutes past noon when there is silence from the opponent? The ball is accelerating across the net and the move is yours. You have two choices. You walk away and hope to do business elsewhere. But, say, your ultimatum was given without much thought and you have no other customer? Your second choice is to go back to the opponent and be greeted with a lower offer - and, why not, in the circumstances you would have acted in a similar manner. The lesson is this - only give an ultimatum when you do not mind whether it is accepted or not. Then, if it is, that`s fine. If not, the terms were so reasonable that you can (hopefully - never a certainty) deal elsewhere. A long-winded or what looked like an abortive transaction has happily been terminated. Move on to profitable business.

AN IMPORTANT REMINDER – NOTHING (GOOD) HAPPENS UNLESS YOU MAKE IT. YOU NOW HAVE FIRMLY IN MIND THAT IT ALL REALLY DOES DEPEND ON YOU.

TWENTY-ONE - WHEN YOU HAVE WHAT YOU SEEK CLOSE THE DEAL. NEVER LINGER. PEOPLE CAN EASILY CHANGE THEIR MINDS

You have within your grasp the desired result. How tempting to push your luck for that little extra. You may succeed. You may not. Is it worth the candle? Why not be shrewd and close the deal before it gets away? That is the action that a sensible negotiator/salesperson always takes. Shake hands and happily move on.

An Aesop Fable vividly illustrates this MA. A chicken laid an egg each day. Its owner doubled its feed so, it was hoped, it would lay two eggs a day. The bird gained weight and stopped laying eggs. Result - the greedy owner lost the one egg a day. The owner wasn`t satisfied and as a result lost all. A lesson to learn and not to forget.

There can be no successful close unless your case has been well-prepared. The way that you attempt to close the deal must follow the pattern you have pursued throughout the negotiations. It is the delicate part of the whole process. Handle it as you would a valuable vase, for once shattered its exact and unspoilt form can never be recreated. If you are too eager to close the deal the opponent may well think, "Hey, what am I giving away. Let`s slow down". He will act cautiously and you could find that the anticipated profitable close has moved away. So, don`t get excited. Treat the close as you have treated the rest of the negotiations. Move carefully, quietly and keep the haggle on a friendly basis. Remember, the best deal is one which both sides consider satisfactory.

WHEN SATISFIED CLOSE THE DEAL

TWENTY-TWO - KEEP NOTES OF MEETINGS, DISCUSSIONS AND ANYTHING OF INTEREST THAT MAY HELP YOU IN THE FUTURE

I bet, like me, you think that you have a good memory. Well, without a note/reminder of some type I would on many occasions have forgotten an important date or event.

I make a brief note immediately after a meeting or a conversation. A few words is sufficient as long as the crucial information is noted. Also, as soon as possible, I diary note dates when actions must be taken. I make a note three or four days before an important event so I have time to prepare a plan, make notes, look-up information, et al. As you look at your diary everyday vital days and information are not missed. Don`t lose the advantage by forgetting. Remember - A SIMPLE NOTE means memory jogged, business done. NO NOTE means a busy person forgets and loses of both business and prestige. It`s as simple as that.

At anytime when a useful thought that could possibly be used in the future comes into mind put it on paper. Note it and it can be considered in the future. Build-up a store of suggestions. I have an "ideas book" and I note ideas and thoughts, otherwise all those gems will be lost.

A reminder - whether you have a good, bad or indifferent memory it can be vastly improved by the aid of notes. The best memory aid in the world does not beat the written note/reminder.

This MA is one of the most important ones. To forget will lose business, business contacts and their faith in you - which will all result in loss of money in the bank and that   proves that you must adopt a sound method so that you do not forget.

TWENTY-THREE - KEEP UP-TO-DATE

Today you may be - probably are - one of the best negotiators/salespersons in town. Yet, next year you may be just an average one earning a run of the mill salary. The quickest way to achieve this downgrade is to become outdated in both your views and your actions. It`s as easy as that.

In these rapidly changing times methods are constantly changing in all working environments. It is so easy to be half-hearted and accept change because it is forced on you by events. That is not the spirit and will mean that you will forever be behind the "in" crowd who are up-to-date and grabbing the business. So, accept the challenge and happily use to your advantage every change as it comes along. Then, you will really know your job and be ready for promotion or the next move. Only by being right up-to-date will you be able to work with true confidence. Remember that principles rarely change, but working methods do - particularly when advertising and PR are concerned. Phrases and words used in the marketplace change and it is important to keep up-to-date in that respect, for to be old-fashioned will put you on the side line. That will lose your business in this fast moving world.

You must know and, as appropriate, use the latest technology - that is vital. Nevertheless, the fundamental golden rules always will apply and you must not get so tied-up in the latest trends that you forget these TWENTY-FIVE MA`s.

This MA is closely linked with MA SIXTEEN - stop, look, listen and observe and you will never be out-of-date.

TO BE OUT-OF-DATE IS TO BE A POTENTIAL LOSER

<u>TWENTY-FOUR</u> - IF IT SEEMS THAT ALL HAS FAILED - LOOK BACK, CONSIDER WHAT TOOK PLACE, LEARN FROM IT AND CONFIDENTLY MOVE ON

You have lost a business deal, been refused a wage rise or whatever. You are depressed. Nothing ever seems to go right. All has failed. Of course, it hasn't - unless you let it be so. It is so easy to write that sentiment and very difficult when dealing with a real life drama. Think along these lines. There are lessons to be learnt. Go back over the episode, isolate and note where you went wrong. In a calm and quiet moment you will realise both the mistake/s made and how you should have acted. That will stick in your mind and (hopefully) you won't make that same mistake again. Your examination will be part of the bank of experience that both good and bad episodes help to create. Don't they say that experience is the sum of both past good and bad mistakes ?

George Orwell wrote, **"No bomb that ever burst, shatters the crystal spirit"**. What a wonderful quote to illustrate clearly this MA. Your unbending aspiration is to succeed. Your desire to work to achieve that and the determination to go forward is your "crystal spirit". To even think that all has failed or is failing is nonsense. Nothing can shatter your "crystal spirit" - only your own self-composed foolishness.

Remember – you never fail, you are learning from the "slings and arrows of outrageous fortune"

TWENTY-FIVE - THESE MA`s APPLY TO OUT OF WORKING HOURS

We know that to be a first-class negotiator/salesperson is a true plus at work. During out of work hours the same rules apply. For negotiating tactics are constantly used. For example, when arguing with your neighbour about a high hedge, with your grocer about the bill, with your garage about the servicing of your car, with the teenage son about his drinking habits... you see, everyday events benefit by knowledge of negotiating/salesmanship. Even if that knowledge has only taught you to be reasonable, sensible and polite I have succeeded!

I DO TRUST THAT YOU HAVE ENJOYED READING ALL OF THESE MANDATORY ACTIONS AND, MORE TO THE POINT, THAT YOU HAVE AND ARE BENEFITTING. I WISH YOU SUCCESS IN THE FUTURE WHEN YOU NEGOTIATE, AND BUY AND SELL.

JOHN MEPHAM